TRINITY
COLLEGE LONDON PRESS

T0081976

INITIAL
KEYBOARDS

Published by
Trinity College London Press Ltd.
trinitycollege.com

Registered in England
Company no. 09726123

Photography by Zute Lightfoot, lightfootphoto.com

Printed in England by Caligraving Ltd.

THE EXAM AT A GLANCE

In your exam you will perform a set of three songs and one of the session skills assessments. You can choose the order of your set list.

SONG 1

Choose a song from this book.

SONG 2

Choose *either* a different song from this book
or a song from the list of additional Trinity Rock & Pop arrangements, available at trinityrock.com
or a song you have chosen yourself: this could be your own cover version or a song that you have written. It should be at the same level as the songs in this book and match the parameters at trinityrock.com

SONG 3: TECHNICAL FOCUS

Song 3 is designed to help you develop specific and relevant techniques in performance. Choose one of the technical focus songs from this book, which cover two specific technical elements.

SESSION SKILLS

Choose *either* **playback** *or* **improvising**.

Session skills are an essential part of every Rock & Pop exam. They are designed to help you develop the techniques music industry performers need.

Sample tests are available in our *Session Skills* books and free examples can be downloaded from trinityrock.com

ACCESS ALL AREAS

GET THE FULL ROCK & POP EXPERIENCE ONLINE AT TRINITYROCK.COM

We have created a range of digital resources to support your learning and give you insider information from the music industry, available online. You will find support, advice and digital content on:

- Songs, performance and technique
- Session skills
- The music industry

You can access tips and tricks from industry professionals featuring:

- Bite-sized videos that include tips from professional musicians on techniques used in the songs
- 'Producer's notes' on the tracks, to increase your knowledge of rock and pop
- Blog posts on performance tips, musical styles, developing technique and advice from the music industry

JOIN US ONLINE AT:

 /TRINITYROCKANDPOP   @TRINITY_ROCK    /TRINITYROCKANDPOP   and at TRINITYROCK.COM

CONTENTS

96 TEARS	4	TECHNICAL FOCUS
ARE 'FRIENDS' ELECTRIC?	10	
BLUE MONDAY	14	TECHNICAL FOCUS
GET LUCKY	18	
THREE LITTLE BIRDS	22	TECHNICAL FOCUS
GIMME SOME LOVIN'	27	
HELLO	31	
SOMETHING TO TALK ABOUT	35	
HELP PAGES	39	

THE AUDIO

Professional demo & backing tracks can be downloaded free, see inside cover for details.

Music preparation and book layout by Andrew Skirrow for Camden Music Services
Music consultants: Nick Crispin, Chris Walters, Christopher Hussey, Julie Parker
Drums recorded by Cab Grant and Jake Watson at AllStar Studios, Chelmsford
All other audio arranged, recorded & produced by Tom Fleming
Keys arrangements: Nigel Fletcher, Simon Foxley, Imogen Hall, Christopher Hussey, Mal Maddock & Jane Watkins

Musicians
Keys, Bass & Guitar: Tom Fleming
Drums: George Double
Vocals: Bo Walton, Brendan Reilly, Alison Symons

INITIAL
KEYBOARDS

SINGLE BY
? & The Mysterians

ALBUM
96 Tears

B-SIDE
Midnight Hour

RELEASED
August 1966

RECORDED
**1966, Bay City
Michigan, USA**

LABEL
**Pa-Go-Go
Cameo-Parkway**

WRITER
Rudy Martinez

PRODUCER
Rudy Martinez

TECHNICAL FOCUS

96 TEARS
? & THE
MYSTERIANS

WORDS AND MUSIC: RUDY MARTINEZ

The '?' in this group's name is the moniker of Mexican-born Rudy Martinez (vocals), frontman of The Mysterians – Robert Balderrama (guitar), Frank Rodriguez (keyboard), Frank Lugo (bass) and Eddie Serrato (drums) – a Michigan-based band whose breakout hit is acknowledged as a classic of garage rock and a forerunner of punk.

'96 Tears' was recorded in Bay City, Michigan in the living room of ? and the Mysterians' manager Lilly Gonzalez, who formed a record label especially for the group. When the song was picked up by a major Detroit radio station it gained a national release via Cameo records and, by October 1966, had knocked the Four Tops' 'Reach Out, I'll Be There' off the top to reach No. 1 (No. 37 in the UK), selling over a million copies in the process. The organ riff, one of the most recognisable in rock, helped define the sound of that era. Often thought to be a Farfisa, the keyboard used was in fact a Vox Continental. The Stranglers released a cover version of the song in 1990 that reached No. 17 in the UK, and in Dave Marsh's acclaimed book *The Heart of Rock and Soul: The 1001 Greatest Singles Ever Made*, the author placed the original version at a fitting No. 96.

TECHNICAL FOCUS

Two technical focus elements are featured in this song:

- Thumb crossing
- Split stave

This song's opening riff includes two changes of position using **thumb crossing**. This will need to be executed smoothly and with precision. At bars 14-17 there is **split stave** writing in the right hand, meaning that your thumb holds sustained notes while the repeating quavers continue above, played by other fingers in the same hand. You'll need to switch immediately into this from the two-note quaver chords in the previous section. If available, an organ sound can be used in this song.

96 TEARS

WORDS AND MUSIC: RUDY MARTINEZ

Garage rock ♩ = 123 (1½ bars count-in)

Lyrics: Too ma-ny tear - drops for one heart to be cry - in'. Too ma-ny tear-

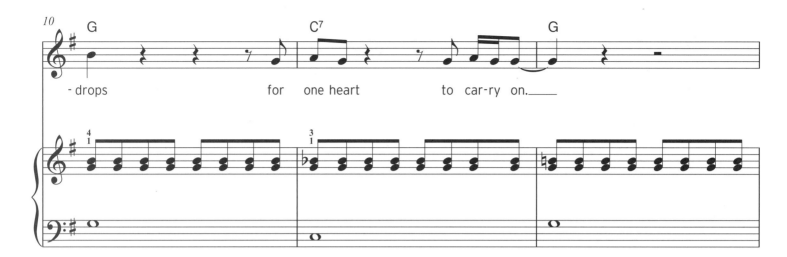

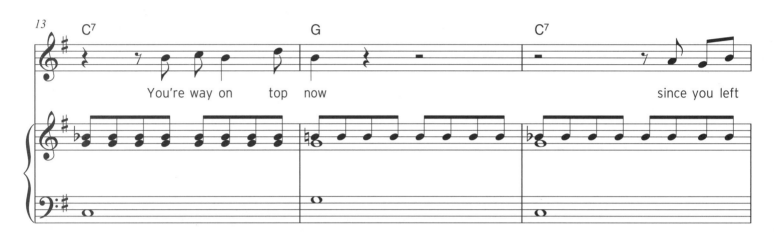

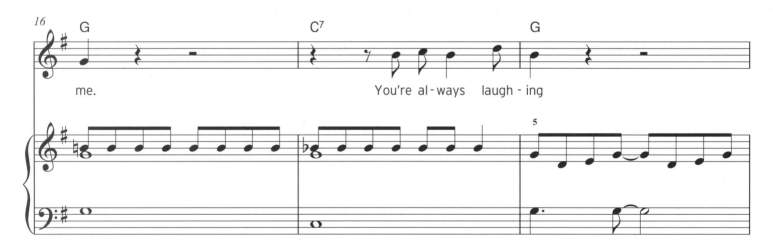

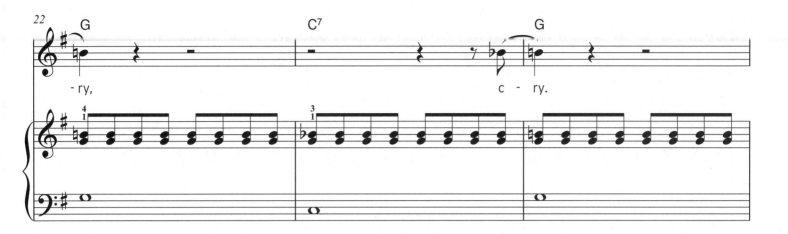

c - ry,   c - ry.

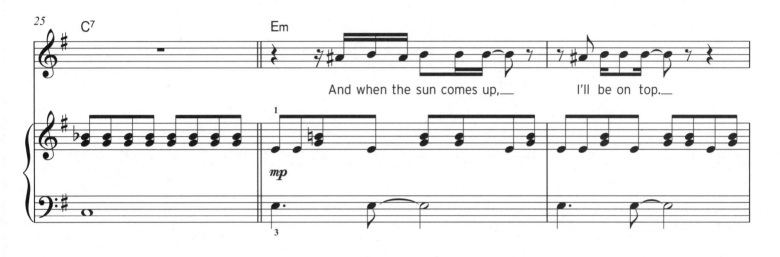

And when the sun comes up,___   I'll be on top.___

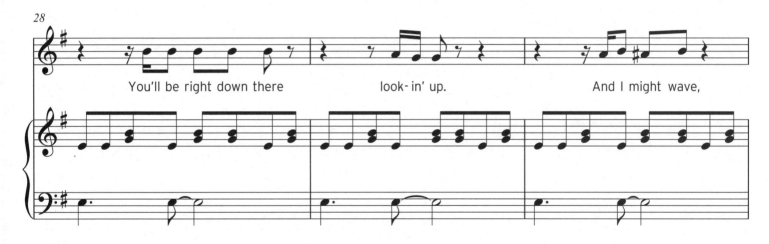

You'll be right down there   look- in' up.   And I might wave,

"Come up here",   but I don't_ see you,___   I will just cry,

cry,____ I'll just cry.

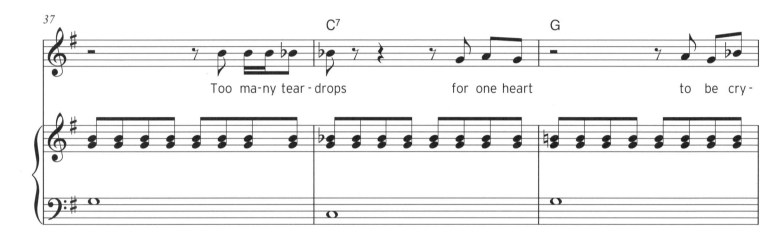

Too ma-ny tear-drops for one heart to be cry-

-in'. Too ma-ny tear-drops for

one heart to car-ry on.____ You're gon-na

INITIAL
KEYBOARDS

SINGLE BY
**Gary Numan
(Tubeway Army)**

ALBUM
Replicas

B-SIDE
We Are So Fragile

RELEASED
19 May 1979

RECORDED
**January–February 1979
Gooseberry Studios
London, England**

LABEL
Beggars Banquet

WRITER
Gary Numan

PRODUCER
Gary Numan

ARE 'FRIENDS' ELECTRIC? GARY NUMAN (TUBEWAY ARMY)

WORDS AND MUSIC: GARY NUMAN

Tubeway Army were formed in London in 1977 by songwriter and musician Gary Numan (vocals, guitar, keyboards) with his uncle Jess Lidyard (drums) and Paul Gardiner (bass). They released their self-titled debut album in 1977, before hitting No. 1 with their influential, synth-heavy second set, 1979's *Replicas*, after which Numan released records under his own name.

The second single from *Replicas*, 'Are "Friends" Electric?' came about when Numan stumbled upon a Minimoog synthesiser in the studio where the band were about to record a more punk-oriented album. This happy discovery led to the instrument becoming the dominant sound of the album, and the single made a huge impact, topping the UK chart for four weeks in 1979. Numan explained the origins of the song:

> I was trying to write two separate songs and I had a verse for one and a chorus for the other. I couldn't finish either, but I realised they sounded alright stuck together. That's why it's five minutes long. Before I recorded it I was playing it back and I hit the wrong note and it sounded much better. That harsh note is probably the crucial note in the hook. It transformed it from almost a ballad into something quite unusual.

In 2002 the track was sampled for Sugababes' No. 1 hit 'Freak Like Me'.

⚡ PERFORMANCE TIPS

This arrangement is based on the original keys part for this song, which means that the vocal line is not included in what you play. You'll need to create a strong, confident groove at the start and, in the section starting at bar 17, smooth and even phrasing between your hands. You can play this song with a synth sound if the instrument you are using has this option.

ARE 'FRIENDS' ELECTRIC?

WORDS AND MUSIC: GARY NUMAN

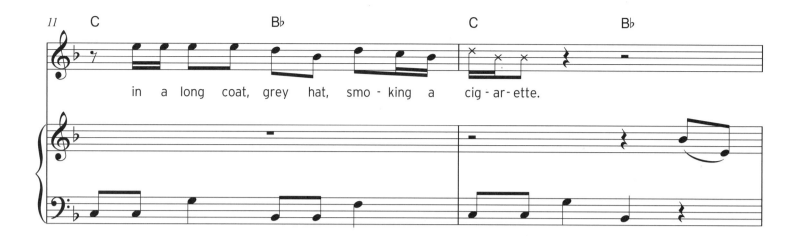

in a long coat, grey hat, smo - king a cig - ar - ette.

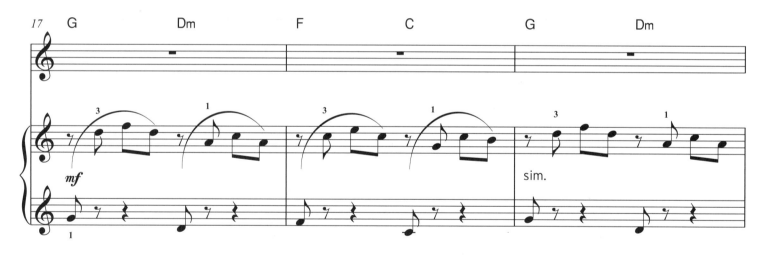

So now I'm a - lone. Now I can think___ for my - self

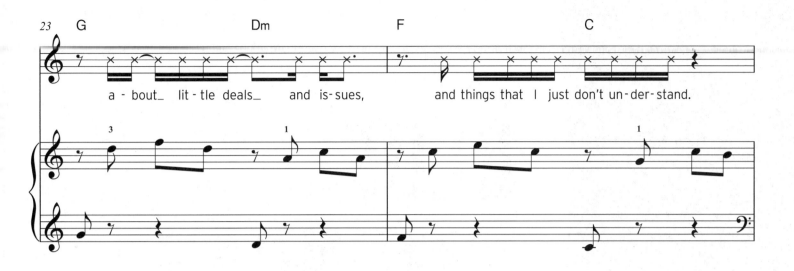

a - bout_ lit - tle deals_ and is - sues, and things that I just don't un - der - stand.

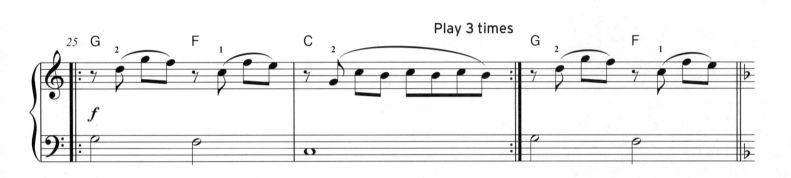

Play 3 times

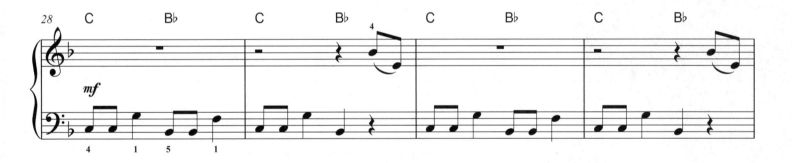

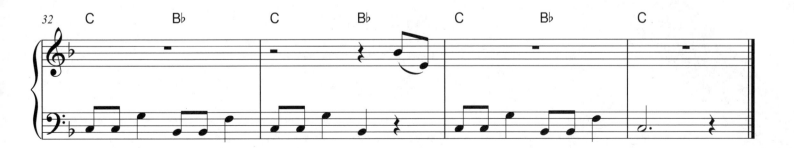

INITIAL
KEYBOARDS

SINGLE BY
New Order

B-SIDE
The Beach

RELEASED
7 March 1983

RECORDED
**1982, Britannia Row
London, England**

LABEL
Factory

WRITERS
**Gillian Gilbert
Peter Hook
Stephen Morris
Bernard Sumner**

TECHNICAL FOCUS

BLUE
MONDAY
NEW ORDER

**WORDS AND MUSIC: GILLIAN GILBERT, PETER HOOK
STEPHEN MORRIS, BERNARD SUMNER**

New Order were formed in Manchester, England in 1980 by former Joy Division members Bernard Sumner (vocals, guitar), Peter Hook (bass) and Stephen Morris (drums) with Gillian Gilbert (keyboards). One of the most acclaimed and influential bands to emerge in the 80s, between 1981 and 2016 they released 11 top-ten albums and 16 top-20 singles in the UK.

Released in March 1983, two months ahead of their second album *Power, Corruption & Lies* (but not included on that album), the seven-and-a-half minute 'Blue Monday' came out as a 12″ vinyl standalone single. By October that year it had made the UK top ten. Utilising early sampler technology, this seminal electronic track went on to become the best-selling 12″ single in music history. Hook explained, 'Bernard and Stephen were the instigators. It was their enthusiasm for new technology.' According to Gilbert:

> The synthesiser melody is slightly out of sync with the rhythm. This was an accident. It was my job to program the entire song from beginning to end, which had to be done manually, by inputting every note. I had the sequence all written down... but I accidentally left a note out, which skewed the melody.

A club classic to this day, *Q Magazine* ranked it at No. 11 in their 1001 Best Songs Ever chart.

TECHNICAL FOCUS

Two technical focus elements are featured in this song:

- Repeating quavers
- Syncopation

This song, which can be played on a synth sound if available, features **repeating quavers** in the left hand starting at bar 9. You'll need to play these evenly, maintaining the pulse as increasingly complex melodic ideas appear in the right hand. The right hand part from bar 41 to the end features **syncopation**, which you'll need to count carefully and perform with accuracy.

TECHNICAL FOCUS
BLUE MONDAY

WORDS AND MUSIC:
GILLIAN GILBERT, PETER HOOK
STEPHEN MORRIS, BERNARD SUMNER

Synthpop ♩ = 130 (2 bars count-in)

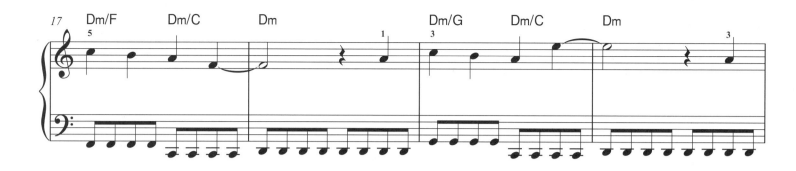

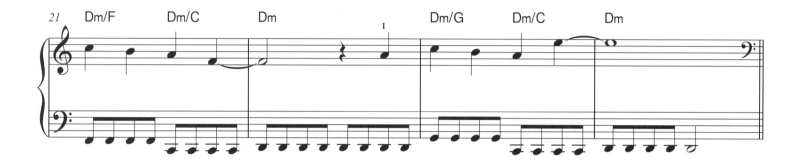

How does it feel___ to treat me like you do?___ When you

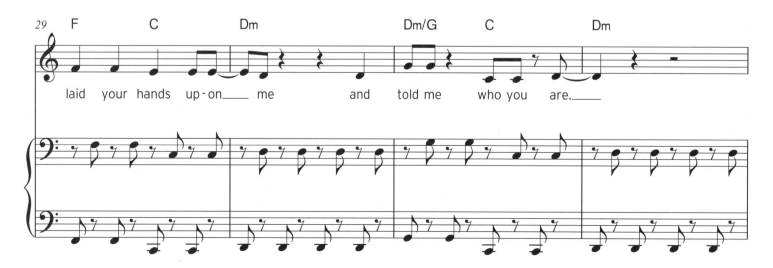

laid your hands up-on___ me and told me who you are.___

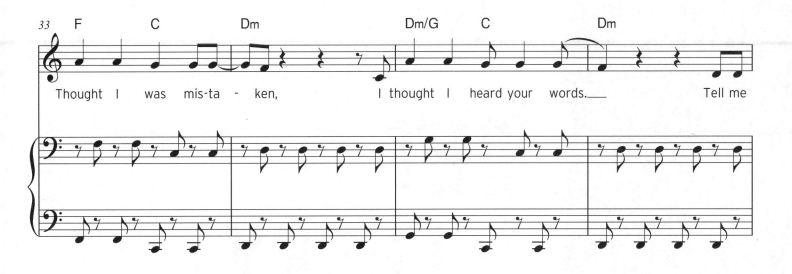

Thought I was mis-ta - ken, I thought I heard your words.___ Tell me

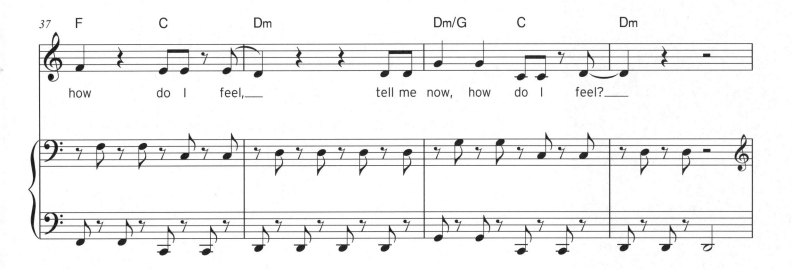

how do I feel,___ tell me now, how do I feel?___

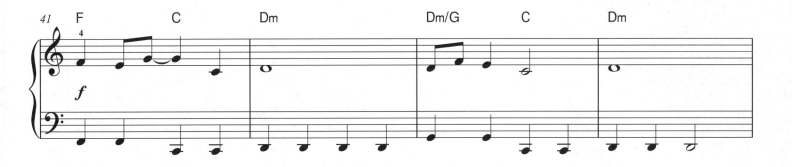

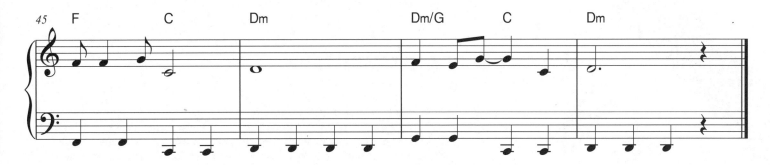

INITIAL
KEYBOARDS

SINGLE BY
Daft Punk

ALBUM
Random Access Memories

B-SIDE
Get Lucky (radio edit)

RELEASED
19 April 2013

RECORDED
2012

LABEL
**Daft Life
Columbia**

WRITERS
**Thomas Bangalter
Guy-Manuel de Homem-Christo
Nile Rodgers
Pharrell Williams**

PRODUCERS
**Thomas Bangalter
Guy-Manuel de Homem-Christo**

GET LUCKY DAFT PUNK

WORDS AND MUSIC: THOMAS BANGALTER, GUY-MANUEL DE HOMEM-CHRISTO, NILE RODGERS, PHARRELL WILLIAMS

French electronic duo Daft Punk first came to the world's attention with their 1995 single 'Da Funk' and 1997 debut album *Homework*, both top-ten hits in the UK. Comprising Thomas Bangalter and Guy-Manuel de Homem-Christo, over the course of four albums the enigmatic, robot-masked pair have become one of the world's biggest dance acts.

'Get Lucky', featuring Pharrell Williams on vocals and Chic's Nile Rodgers on guitar, was released as the lead single from Daft Punk's fourth studio album, 2013's US and UK No. 1 *Random Access Memories*. It swiftly hit No. 1 in numerous countries including the UK, selling over nine million copies worldwide. In the US it reached No. 2 for five weeks, held off the top by Robin Thicke's 'Blurred Lines' which also featured Williams. When Daft Punk first played Rodgers their demo of the song, he began experimenting with different guitar parts to find the right groove until he saw 'both guys smiling. Then I thought, OK, I'm there.' Williams came up with the lyrics and recorded his vocal at the French duo's Paris studio. Daft Punk won four Grammy Awards in 2014, including Album of the Year and Record of the Year for 'Get Lucky'.

⚡ PERFORMANCE TIPS

This arrangement is mostly an accompaniment part, except for one section where you play the melody. Starting at bar 13, this passage requires several shifts of right hand position, which you'll need to manage while maintaining a smooth phrasing style. You'll also need a strong feeling for the pulse throughout, keeping a grooving crotchet beat in your left hand. If you have access to an electric piano sound, you could consider using it in this song.

GET LUCKY

WORDS AND MUSIC:

THOMAS BANGALTER, GUY-MANUEL DE HOMEM-CHRISTO
NILE RODGERS, PHARRELL WILLIAMS

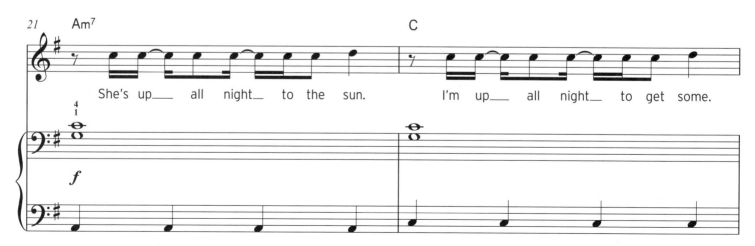

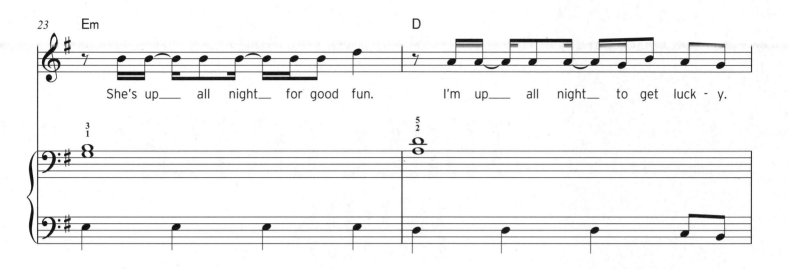

She's up___ all night___ for good fun. I'm up___ all night___ to get luck-y.

We're up___ all night___ to the sun. We're up___ all night___ to get some.

We're up___ all night___ for good fun. We're up___ all night___ to get luck-y.

mf

INITIAL
KEYBOARDS

SINGLE BY
Bob Marley & The Wailers

ALBUM
Exodus

B-SIDE
Every Need Got an Ego to Feed

RELEASED
3 June 1977 (album)
12 September 1980 (single)

RECORDED
1976, Harry J Studio Kingston, Jamaica

January-April 1977 Island Studios, London England (album)

LABEL
Tuff Gong
Island Records

WRITER
Bob Marley

PRODUCERS
Bob Marley & The Wailers

TECHNICAL FOCUS

THREE LITTLE BIRDS
BOB MARLEY & THE WAILERS

WORDS AND MUSIC: BOB MARLEY

Bob Marley was a Jamaican singer-songwriter and reggae artist who started out as a member of The Wailers with Bunny Wailer and Peter Tosh. The latter two left in 1974, and Marley continued with longstanding rhythm section Aston Barrett (bass) and Carlton Barrett (drums) to become the most successful reggae act of all time.

The penultimate song on Bob Marley and the Wailers' ninth album, 1977's *Exodus*, 'Three Little Birds' wasn't actually released as a single until 1980. Three further albums had been released in the interim: 1978's *Kaya*, 1979's *Survival* and 1980's *Uprising*. It was the fourth of five top-30 hit singles from *Exodus*, following on from 'Waiting in Vain', 'Jamming' and the title track, reaching No. 17 in the UK. It was his last hit while still alive (Marley died in 1981 at the age of 36). One of the song's inspirations came from Marley's backing singers I Threes, comprising his wife Rita Marley, Marcia Griffiths and Judy Mowatt, whom he referred to as 'my three little birds'. Three years after his death, the song featured on Marley's greatest hits collection *Legend*, his first No. 1 album in the UK and a multi-million seller that remains the world's best-ever selling reggae album.

TECHNICAL FOCUS

Two technical focus elements are featured in this song:

- Offbeat rhythm
- Articulation

The reggae style of this song presents specific challenges. One of these is the **offbeat rhythm** of the chords with infrequent downbeats, requiring a strong sense of internal pulse. The **articulation** of the chords, particularly the contrast between staccato and tenuto starting at bar 21, is also stylistically important. This song sounds good with an organ sound if available.

TECHNICAL FOCUS

THREE LITTLE BIRDS

WORDS AND MUSIC: BOB MARLEY

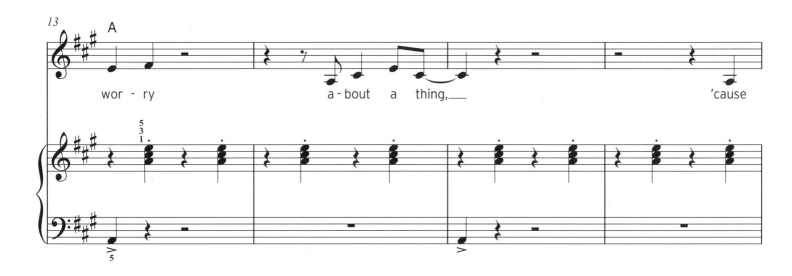

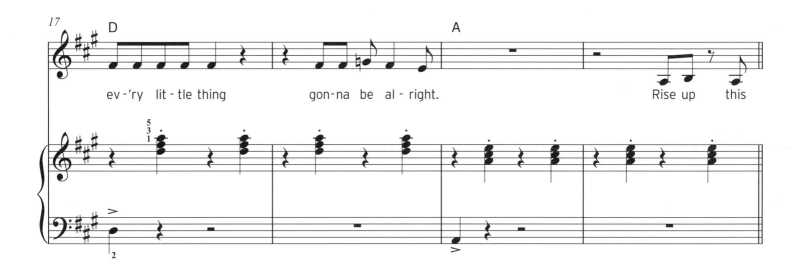

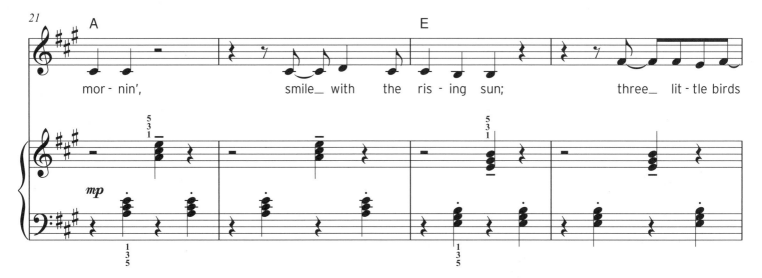

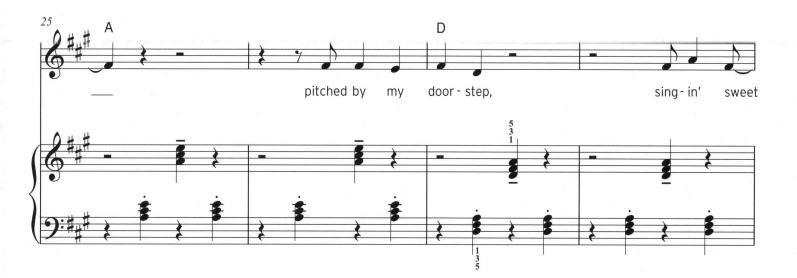

pitched by my door-step, sing-in' sweet

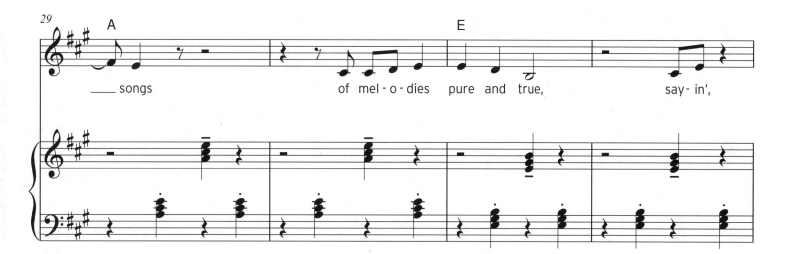

songs of mel-o-dies pure and true, say-in',

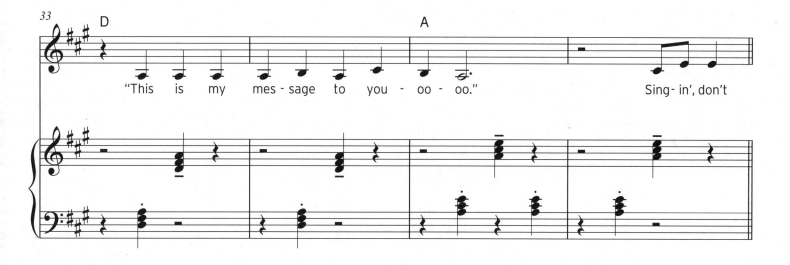

"This is my mes-sage to you - oo - oo." Sing-in', don't

wor - ry   a-bout   a   thing,____   'cause

ev - 'ry   lit - tle thing   gon - na be al - right.

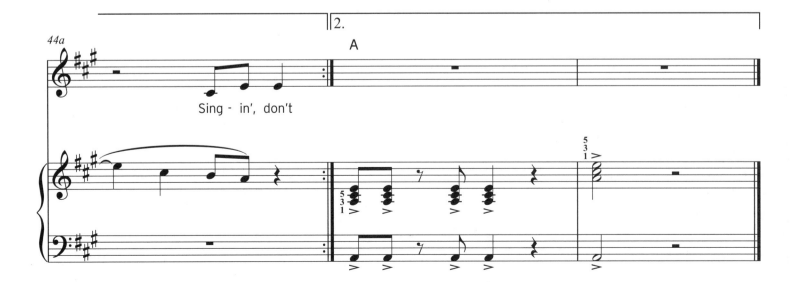

Sing - in', don't

GIMME SOME LOVIN' THE SPENCER DAVIS GROUP

WORDS AND MUSIC: STEVE WINWOOD, SPENCER DAVIS MUFF WINWOOD

SINGLE BY
The Spencer Davis Group

B-SIDE
Blues in F

RELEASED
October 1966

LABEL
**Fontana (UK)
United Artists (USA)**

WRITERS
**Steve Winwood
Spencer Davis
Muff Winwood**

PRODUCERS
**Chris Blackwell
Jimmy Miller**

The Spencer Davis Group was formed in Birmingham, England in 1963, by Steve Winwood (vocals, guitar, keyboard), Spencer Davis (guitar, vocals), Muff Winwood (bass) and Pete York (drums). The band was most successful between 1965 and 1967, during which period their first three albums reached the UK top ten.

Heavily influenced by Homer Banks' song 'A Lot of Love', 'Gimme Some Lovin'' was written by Steve Winwood on the Hammond B-3 organ when he was 17 years old. It almost became the band's third No. 1 hit in the UK but peaked at No. 2 in November 1966 behind The Beach Boys' 'Good Vibrations'. The previous year they had hit No. 1 with the singles 'Keep on Running' and 'Somebody Help Me', both written by the Jamaican musicians and songwriter Jackie Edwards. With its American R&B-fuelled sound, 'Gimme Some Lovin'' was aimed at cracking the US market and succeeded in becoming the band's first top-ten hit there. Their follow-up, 'I'm a Man', was the group's final top-ten hit both in the UK and US, before both Winwood brothers left to pursue different musical ventures. Steve found particular success, first with the bands Traffic and Blind Faith and then a long-running solo career.

⚡ PERFORMANCE TIPS

This accompaniment-based keys arrangement will suit you if you have an octave stretch in your left hand, though the octave leaps can be lightly detached and grooving rather than smooth. The crotchet triplets in bar 2 will need careful timing, and the right-hand chords starting at bar 19 will need precision to manage the position shift in every bar. You might like to use an organ sound for this song if you have one available.

GIMME SOME LOVIN'

WORDS AND MUSIC: STEVE WINWOOD
SPENCER DAVIS, MUFF WINWOOD

Well, my temp - 'ra - ture's ri - sing and my feet left the floor,___ cra - zy peo - ple knock - in' 'cause they're

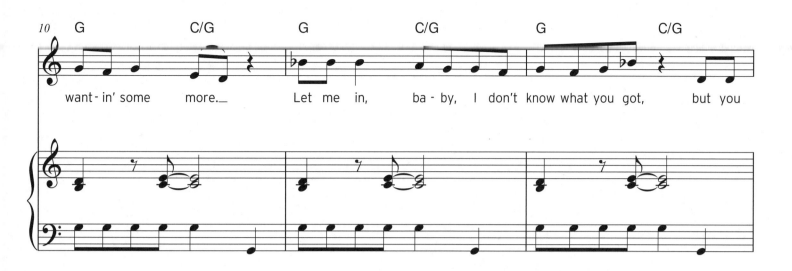

want - in' some   more.___   Let me in,   ba - by,   I don't know what you got,   but you

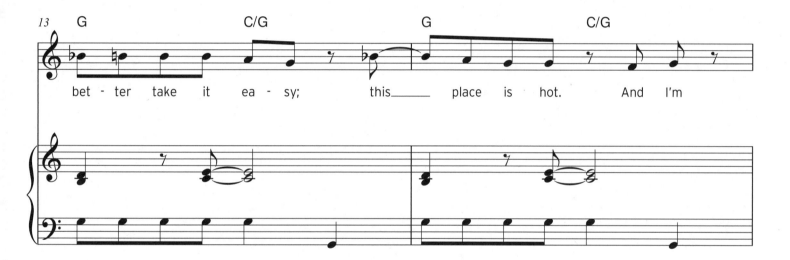

bet - ter take it ea - sy;   this___ place is hot.   And I'm

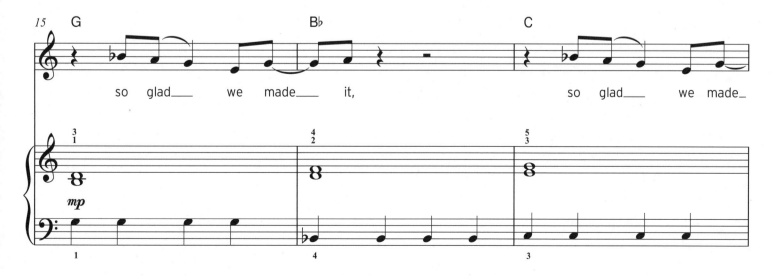

*so glad___ we made___ it,   so glad___ we made_*

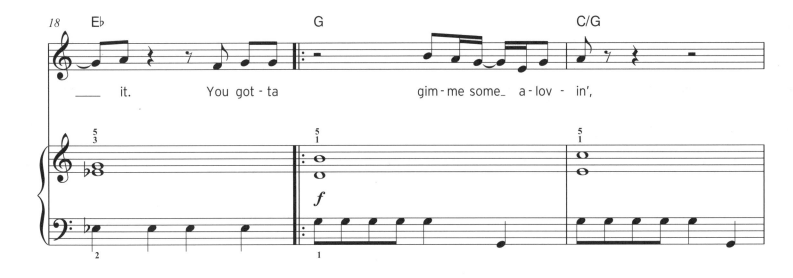

it. You got-ta gim-me some_ a-lov-in',

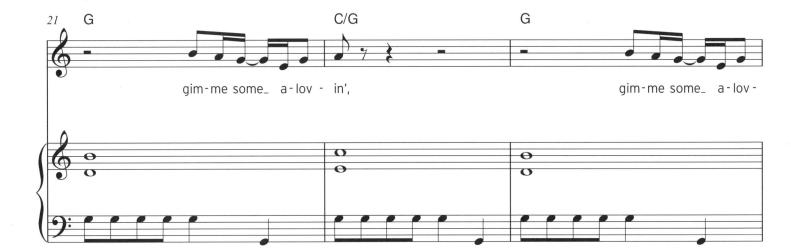

gim-me some_ a-lov-in', gim-me some_ a-lov-

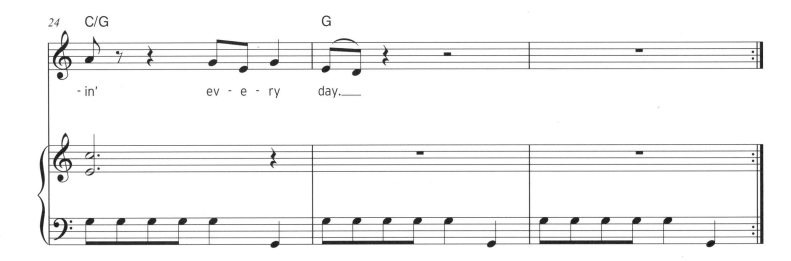

-in' ev-e-ry day.___

HELLO
ADELE

WORDS AND MUSIC: ADELE, GREG KURSTIN

SINGLE BY
Adele

ALBUM
25

RELEASED
23 October 2015

RECORDED
**2014-2015
Metroplolis Studios
London, England**

LABEL
XL Recordings

WRITERS
**Adele
Greg Kurstin**

PRODUCER
Greg Kurstin

The English singer-songwriter Adele was born in north London and graduated from the city's BRIT School, a launchpad for several well-known artists including Amy Winehouse. In a remarkable first decade, Adele would become one of the best-selling artists of all-time, with worldwide sales of over 100 million and the recipient of Brit Awards, Grammy Awards, Golden Globes and an Oscar.

'Hello' marked the return of Adele after a three-year hiatus, released in October 2015, one month ahead of her third album *25*. The song reached No. 1 in almost every country it charted in and became the first song in the US to sell over a million copies digitally within a week of its release. Co-writer and producer Greg Kurstin revealed one of the song's influences: 'We talked about Tom Waits and different storytellers like that. I think that was the idea, that we wanted to do something that was very honest about where she was at right now, and she wanted to do something that was real and believable.' There was a six-month gap between writing the verses and the chorus. 'We had half a song written. I just had to be very patient,' said Kurstin.

⚡ PERFORMANCE TIPS

This accompaniment arrangement shows just how straightforward a hit song can be. Its signature repeating rhythmic pattern is featured in many piano ballads and continues with minimal variation throughout, so you'll need to play it accurately and consistently. There are also some dynamic contrasts to look out, especially the drop from *f* to *mp* near the end. A piano sound should be used, reflecting the acoustic piano of the original.

HELLO

WORDS AND MUSIC:

ADELE, GREG KURSTIN

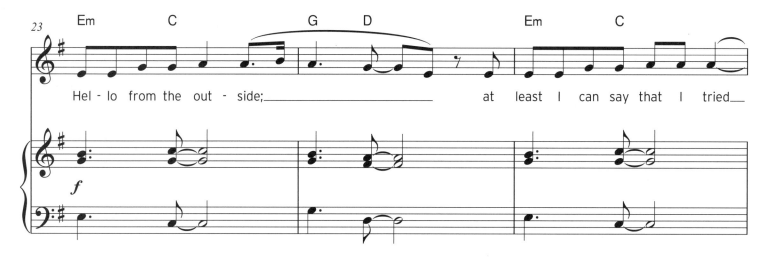

Hel - lo from the out - side;_____ at least I can say that I tried__

_____ to tell you____ I'm sor - ry____ for

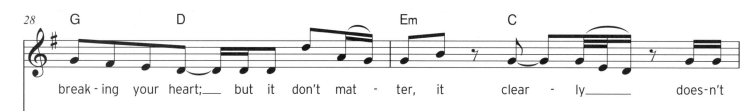

break - ing your heart;___ but it don't mat - ter, it clear - ly____ does-n't

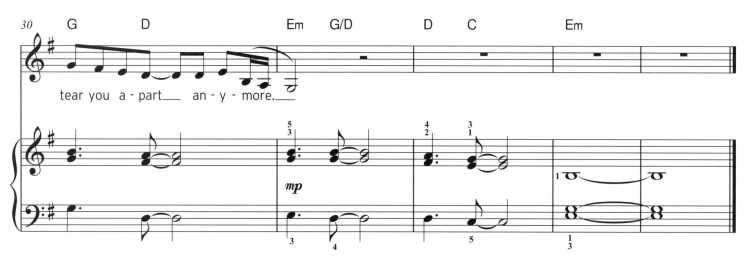

tear you a - part___ an - y - more.___

SOMETHING TO TALK ABOUT

BADLY DRAWN BOY

WORDS AND MUSIC: DAMON GOUGH

SINGLE BY
Badly Drawn Boy

ALBUM
About a Boy

B-SIDE
Walk in the Park with Angie

Hamster Countdown

Something to Talk About

RELEASED
8 April 2002 (album)
10 June 2002 (single)

RECORDED
2001
Larrabee East, Third Stone
Recording & Cello Studios
Los Angeles, California
USA

AIR Studios, London
England (album)

LABEL
Twisted Nerve
XL Recordings

WRITER
Damon Gough

PRODUCERS
Badly Drawn Boy
Tom Rothrock

Badly Drawn Boy is the stage name of Manchester singer-songwriter Damon Gough, whose debut 2000 album *The Hour of Bewilderbeast* won that year's Mercury Music Prize. The album caught the attention of British author Nick Hornby, who asked Gough to score the film adaptation of his novel *About a Boy*.

Taken from the soundtrack to *About a Boy,* a 2002 comedy starring Hugh Grant and a 12-year-old Nicholas Hoult, 'Something to Talk About' was the second single to be released from the No. 6 UK hit album. The album was produced and mixed by Tom Rothrock, who had worked on the commercial breakthrough albums by two American artists often compared at the time with Badly Drawn Boy: Elliott Smith and Beck. Joey Waronker, who played drums on albums by both Beck and Elliott Smith, also plays drums on 'Something to Talk About' (as well as the album's first single 'Silent Sigh'). Two months after the soundtrack's release, 'Something to Talk About' reached No. 28 on the UK singles chart.

⚡ PERFORMANCE TIPS

This arrangement contains several contrasting musical ideas, and to play it well you'll need to be confident in switching between different styles. The song is swung, which means that the quaver pairs need a laid-back feel – listen to the original to get a sense of the right approach here. Both hands feature changes of position, requiring care, and the melody in bars 19, 23 and 26-27 should be smoothly phrased. A piano sound is recommended.

SOMETHING TO TALK ABOUT

WORDS AND MUSIC:
DAMON GOUGH

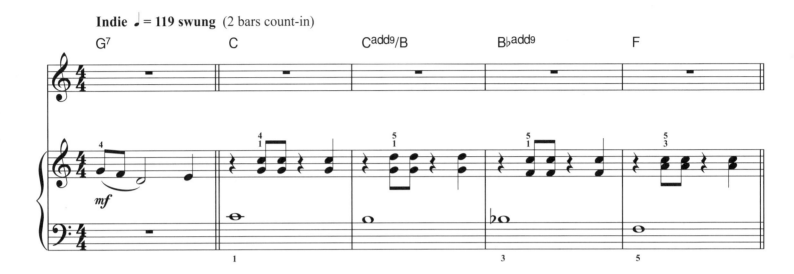

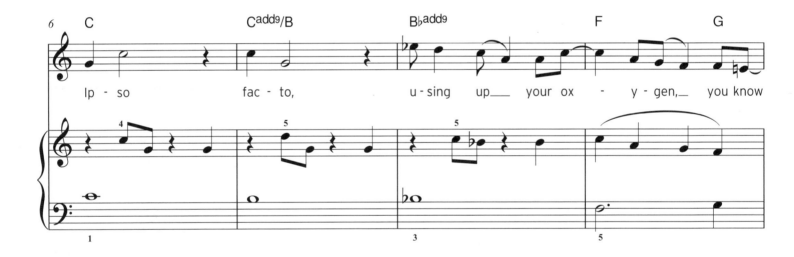

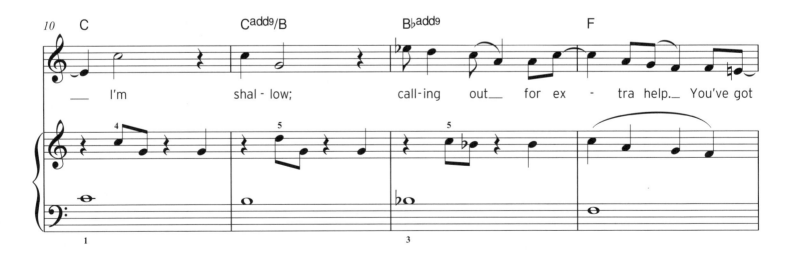

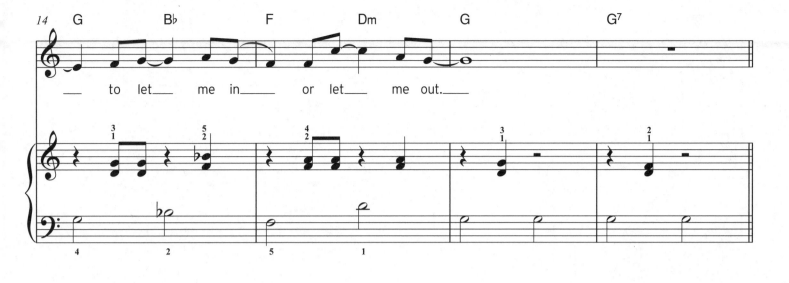

_14_ G ... Bb ... F ... Dm ... G ... G7

___ to let___ me in___ or let___ me out.___

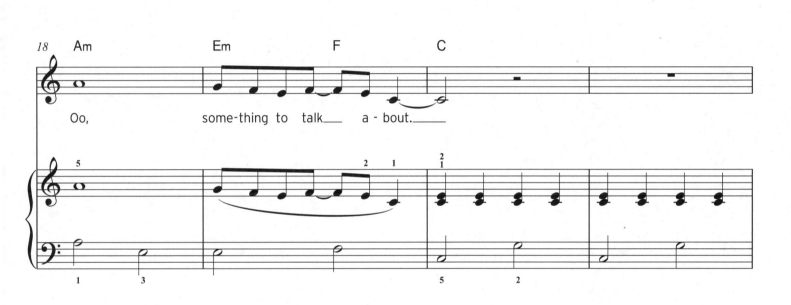

_18_ Am ... Em ... F ... C

Oo, ... some-thing to talk___ a - bout.___

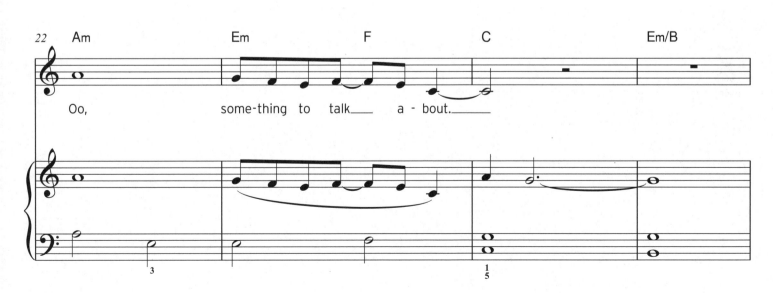

_22_ Am ... Em ... F ... C ... Em/B

Oo, ... some-thing to talk___ a - bout.___

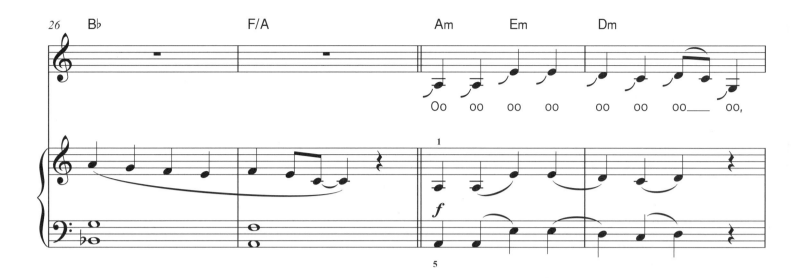

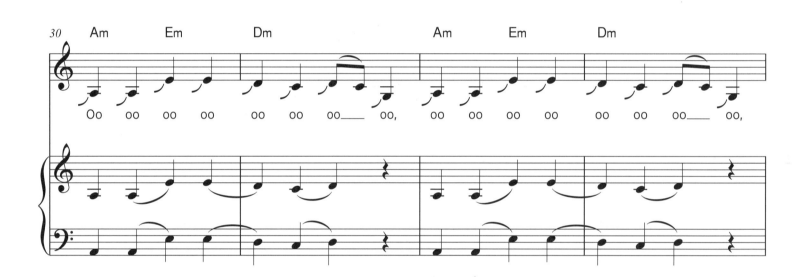

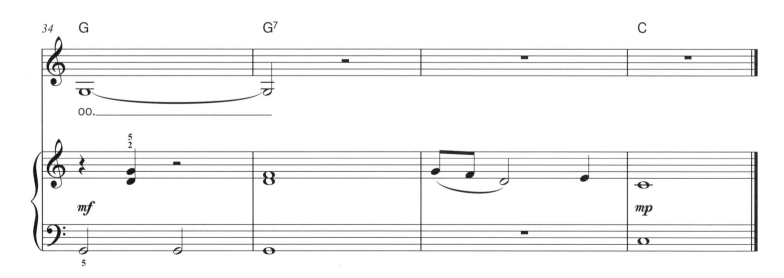

PLAYING WITH BACKING TRACKS

All your backing tracks can be downloaded from soundwise.co.uk

- The backing tracks begin with a click track, which sets the tempo and helps you start accurately

- Be careful to balance the volume of the backing track against your instrument

- Listen carefully to the backing track to ensure that you are playing in time

- Keyboard players should not use auto-accompaniment features for these exams as the aim is to play with a backing track

If you are creating your own backing track, here are some further tips:

- Make sure that the sound quality is of a good standard

- Think carefully about the instruments/sounds you are using on the backing track

- Avoid copying what you are playing in the exam on the backing track – it should support, not duplicate

- Do you need to include a click track at the beginning?

COPYRIGHT IN A SONG

If you are a singer, instrumentalist or songwriter it is important to know about copyright. When someone writes a song they automatically own the copyright (sometimes called 'the rights'). Copyright begins once a piece of music has been documented or recorded (eg by video, CD or score notation) and protects the interests of the creators. This means that others cannot copy it, sell it, make it available online or record it without the owner's permission or the appropriate licence.

COVER VERSIONS

- When an artist creates a new version of a song it is called a 'cover version'

- The majority of songwriters subscribe to licensing agencies, also known as 'collecting societies'. When a songwriter is a member of such an agency, the performing rights to their material are transferred to the agency (this includes cover versions of their songs)

- The agency works on the writer's behalf by issuing licences to performance venues, who report what songs have been played, which in turn means that the songwriter will receive a payment for any songs used

- You can create a cover version of a song and use it in an exam without needing a licence

There are different rules for broadcasting (eg TV, radio, internet), selling or copying (pressing CDs, DVDs etc), and for printed material, and the appropriate licences should be sought out.

CHOOSING SONGS FOR YOUR EXAM

SONG 1

Choose a song from this book.

SONG 2

Choose a song which is:

Either a different song from this book

or from the list of additional Trinity Rock & Pop arrangements, available at trinityrock.com

or from a printed or online source

or your own arrangement

or a song that you have written yourself

You can play Song 2 unaccompanied or with a backing track (minus the keyboard part). If you like, you can create a backing track yourself (or with friends), add your own vocals, or be accompanied live by another musician.

The level of difficulty and length of the song should be similar to the songs in this book and match the parameters available at trinityrock.com

When choosing a song, think about:

- Does it work on my instrument?
- Are there any technical elements that are too difficult for me? (If so, perhaps save it for when you do the next grade)
- Do I enjoy playing it?
- Does it work with my other songs to create a good set list?

SONG 3: TECHNICAL FOCUS

Song 3 is designed to help you develop specific and relevant techniques in performance. Choose one of the technical focus songs from this book, which cover two specific technical elements.

SHEET MUSIC

If your choice for Song 2 is not from this book, you must provide the examiner with a photocopy. The title, writers of the song and your name should be on the sheet music. You must also bring an original copy of the book, or a download version with proof of purchase, for each song that you perform in the exam.

Your music can be:

- A lead sheet with lyrics, chords and melody line
- A chord chart with lyrics
- A full score using conventional staff notation